MALTA
GOZO AND COMINO

Miller Distributors Limited
Miller House, Airport Way, Tarxien Road, Luqa LQA 05 Malta.
P.O. Box 25, Malta International Airport LQA 05 Malta.
Telephone: (356) 21 66 44 88 Fax (356) 21 67 67 99
info@millermalta.com   www.millermalta.com

Editorial management: Monica Bonechi
Graphic design, picture research
and cover: Sonia Gottardo
Layout: Sonia Gottardo
Maps: Stefano Benini

The photographs belong to the archive of
Casa Editrice Bonechi
and were taken by Andrea Fantauzzo.
Other sources: Archivio Plurigraf, Kevin Casha,
Daniel Borg, Jonathan Beacom & Perfecta Advertising.
The photographs on pages 37 centre left, 47 top and
48 are by Hubert Cini and are kindly provided by Miller
Distributors Limited. The photos of the Gozo Cathedral
(p. 64 bottom and p. 65 top left) were taken and printed
by the courtesy of the Cathedral Chapter.

The publisher will be grateful for information concerning
the sources of photographs without credits and will be
pleased to acknowledge them in future editions.

© Copyright 2008
by CASA EDITRICE PERSEUS - PLURIGRAF collection
Published and printed by
Centro Stampa Editoriale Bonechi,
Sesto Fiorentino (FI)

Introduction

The Republic of Malta is located in the centre of the Mediterranean Sea. The archipelago is formed of two main islands, Malta and Gozo which, as well as Comino, are the only inhabited islands, and some smaller uninhabited islands named Cominotto, Filfla and St Paul. Thanks to its position, Malta has represented a bridge between Europe and Africa since ancient times. The islands are in fact only 90 kilometres from Sicily and 290 from the African coast. With a population of about 400,000 inhabitants and a surface area of 320 km², Malta has the highest density of population per square kilometre of any European country. Numerous peoples have occupied these islands in the course of its lengthy history (Phoenicians, Romans, Arabs, Normans, Spanish, French and English) leaving behind an artistic and cultural heritage of immense value. As early as prehistoric times large temples were built indicating a highly developed and sophisticated civilization. It was, however, under the Order of the Knights of Saint John that Malta developed culturally and artistically and the island

was enhanced with beautiful palaces, churches, fortifications and works of art. With its mild climate, clear sea, impressive cliffs and the bright colours of the Mediterranean shrubs, this group of islands is a true paradise and an ideal destination for holidays of all kinds. The Maltese have traces of all the various peoples who have occupied Malta and combine the traits of many ethnic groups, although characteristic Semitic and Anglo-Saxon features are predominant. Most of the population is, however, of Arab descent. The Catholic religion is practised by 90 per cent of the inhabitants.

The official languages are Maltese and English. The former is of Semitic origin and the vocabulary contains a wealth of words with neo-Latin and Anglo-Saxon origins. There are numerous instances of the Arab influence, which lasted some 300 years, especially in the grammatical structure of the language, as well as in the vocabulary. Italian was the official language of the Knights of the Order of St John and until 1934 also of culture and the ruling classes and is therefore still quite common today.

MALTA

When Grand Master Jean Parisot de la Valette laid the foundation stone of Humilissima Civitas Vallettae, *the last thing that he had in mind was a city of fine palaces. Valletta was intended as a fortress to protect the two harbours on either side of the rocky peninsula on which it was to be built. According to tradition, the Church of Our Lady of Victories was built over the foundation stone itself. The façade of the church was altered in 1690 but is otherwise unchanged.*

An aerial view clearly showing the impressive defensive structures that encircle Valletta. In the centre, on either side of the City Gate are St James' Bastion (right) and St John's Cavalier (left).

VALLETTA

The urban centre of Valletta is surrounded and protected by ancient city walls with imposing ramparts that represent not only the main structure of a complex defensive system but also a splendid and perfect example of the most advanced 15th-century military engineering; the arrangement and development of the town road system and layout is still inevitably influenced by these defensive structures and their conservation has lead to the recognition of the capital of Malta as a Cultural Heritage site.

St James' Bastion extends wedge-like in the direction of nearby Floriana and the two mighty defensive fortifications are actually connected.

Below the rampart is a ditch and in 1640 plans were made to widen and deepen this, transforming it into a navigable canal which would have linked the Grand Harbour to Marsamxett. The plan never became a reality but is evidence of the importance that the Maltese always attributed to the town's system of fortifications.

Behind St James' Bastion are further defensive buildings used in the past as munitions and gunpowder deposits and as safe storage for the artillery. Of particular note are *St James' Cavalier* and *St John's Cavalier*, also known as St John's Bastion where, since 1968, the Embassy of the Sovereign Military Hospitaller Order of St John of Jerusalem, of Rhodes and Malta is housed.

THE CITY GATE

A visit to Valletta must certainly begin at the City Gate, the real entrance to the city, built in 1964 over a pre-existing gate and destined to provide a grandiose access to the centre of Valletta which is today almost entirely a pedestrian area. Just through the Gate lies *Freedom Square* where *Republic Street* begins, but a wide open space precedes this which, when Floriana was founded, was kept unencumbered in order to provide a clear range for firing the city's defensive artillery. Today this large square is almost constantly full of buses and in the centre stands the **Triton Fountain**, a 20th-century work by the Maltese sculptor, Vincent Apap.

Views of the Upper Barracca Gardens from where, in addition to the row of cannons known as the Saluting Battery, Fort St Angelo can be seen; the old Castile Rampart where the Lower Barracca Gardens now are; the Doric temple which stands here is dedicated to Sir Alexander Ball (below).

UPPER AND LOWER BARRACCA GARDENS

When the mighty defensive ramparts of Valletta's city walls ceased to have a protective function and effectively took on a more urban role, the improvement and enhancement of their appearance became a matter of urgency. Thus this extensive area was quickly reorganised and the artillery, which until then had occupied the area, gave way to tranquil and luxuriant gardens. In one part the Upper Barracca Gardens came into being and were originally the favourite spot of the Italian Knights. There is a magnificent view across the Three Cities and the Grand Harbour. In the other section and also overlooking the Grand Harbour are the Lower Barracca Gardens which, built on what was once the Castile Rampart, extend towards Senglea and Vittoriosa not far away.

REPUBLIC STREET

The true centre of La Valetta is without any doubt Republic Street, the longest, widest and most typical of the city. A fascinating pedestrian area stretching from the City Gate to Fort St Elmo, the most prestigious shops, the most important offices, and numerous monumental buildings are located on this important street. Thus, beside the *Auberge de Provence* and the *Grand Master's Palace* right at the beginning of Republic Street at the City Gate end, stand two important churches: the 18th-century **Church of St Barbara**, and the **Church of St Francis.**

Right, a lively and constant crowd of Maltese and tourists in Republic Street.

Left, Old Theatre Street.

MERCHANTS STREET

While Republic Street is the place to go shopping, parallel to it and just as crowded and busy, Merchants Street is clearly the home of the market. Held here every morning it attracts numerous visitors and provides products of all kinds, including an amazing variety of clothing. In the shadow of the traditional wooden balconies there are also many crafts shops where the characteristic filigree is produced as well as terracotta, and items of blown glass. There are also famous buildings here, such as the **Auberge d'Italie**, built in the 16th century with one floor only, and **Palazzo Parisio** where Napoleon stayed in 1798.

AUBERGE DE CASTILLE

The Auberge de Castille, Leon and Portugal, is the largest and perhaps finest of all the Auberges and belonged to the Spanish and Portugese "Langues". Its head was the Grand Chancellor of the Order of St John.
It was first built in 1574 by Gerolamo Cassar on a site originally intended for the Magistrates Palace. Extensive reconstruction was undertaken in 1744 during Grand Master Pinto de Fonseca's term of office.
Domenico Cachia, the architect responsible for these modifications, was influenced by the Prefecture in Lecce and produced a very imposing façade.
Now the prime minister's residence, one of the most impressive features of this building is the large stairway leading from the ground to the first floor, as well as the courtyard, flanked on three sides by an austere portico.

The Auberges of the Knights

The Order of the Knights was divided into "Langues" (from 'language' indicating nationality), each of which had an Auberge, as their residence was known, with a chapel, dining hall and other rooms arranged around a courtyard. Originally there were eight Auberges all located in Vittoriosa. When Valletta came into being Auberges were constructed there too – but only seven, as Henry VIII had suppressed the English "Langue" following a dispute with the Pope and consequently the English Knights did not have a residence of their own in the new city. The Auberges were all built by Gerolamo Cassar between 1571 and 1590. Today only five still remain: the Auberge d'Italie in Merchants Street which now also houses the Malta Tourist Authority, the Auberge de Provence in Republic Street, the Auberge d'Aragon, the oldest and simplest structure, the Auberge d'Angleterre et Bavière and the Auberge de Castille.

AUBERGE DE PROVENCE (ARCHAEOLOGICAL MUSEUM)

The Auberge de Provence was built between 1571 and 1575 to a design by the Maltese architect Gerolamo Cassar. The façade was altered during the first half of the 17th century and its appearance has remained unchanged, with characteristic Doric columns on the ground level, and Ionic pillars on the first floor. The Auberge was the residence of the "Langue" de Provence, its Head, the "Grand Commandeur" being the Treasurer of the Order. From 1820 to 1954 the building housed the British officers' Union Club and following a complete programme of restoration carried out in 1990 it now houses the **National Museum of Archaeology**. This fascinating museum, with its quite unique patrimony of Maltese archaeological items, houses a valuable collection of prehistoric artefacts such as pottery, statuettes (including ten headless statues of fertility goddesses), stone implements, personal and other ornaments recovered from Malta's prehistoric and megalithic temple sites. Several models of these temples are on permanent display.

Opposite page, the austere façade of the Auberge de Castille.
Above, the exterior of the Auberge de Provence and on the right, one of the rooms in the National Archaeological Museum.

A view of the splendid light classical interior of the Museum of Fine Arts and one of the works of art exhibited there.

NATIONAL MUSEUM OF FINE ARTS

South Street is one of the most elegant streets in the city and one of the most graceful palaces located here is *Admiralty House* home to the National Museum of Fine Arts. This was one of the first buildings erected in Valletta, but it was rebuilt in its present form between 1761 and 1765. It houses paintings, sculpture, furniture and objects connected with the Order of St John. The permanent collection includes works by Reni, Valentini, Stomer, Preti, Tiepolo, Favray and Perugino. A section is specially reserved for works by Maltese artists. Temporary exhibitions and lectures are also held here.

The solemn façade
of St John's Co-Cathedral
and a detail of the bell tower.

ST. JOHN'S
CO-CATHEDRAL

In 1573 Grand Master Jean de la Cassière authorized the construction of a conventual church of the Order of St John. It was completed in 1578 by the Maltese architect Gerolamo Cassar. Its austere exterior gives no indication of the opulent and extravagant interior. A modest portico over the main door supports the balcony used by the Grand Master to present himself to the public after election. The rectangular baroque **interior** was embellished by successive Grand Masters and further enriched by the "Gioja" or gift, which every Knight was bound by statute to give on admission to the

Left, the sumptuous interior of St John's Co-Cathedral.

The Beheading of Saint John the Baptist

The only work to have been signed by Caravaggio and by far the largest (oil on canvas, 361 x 520 cm.), the *Beheading of St John the Baptist* was painted in 1608 for the Oratory of the Co-Cathedral and earned the artist the award of the Maltese Cross. But an instinctive despondency seems to pervade both his painting and himself: the backgrounds are sombre, dark and shadowy and the brushstrokes increasingly rapid. The overall impression is of a dramatic force represented by the device of the Saint's blood which flows into the artist's signature in red; the figure of John the Baptist lying on the ground is a powerful element in the entire structure of the scene, where the dark and austere setting dominates the expressive and tragic participation of the figures.

Order. Between 1662-1667, Mattia Preti "Il Calabrese" painted the *Life of St John the Baptist*, patron saint of the Order, directly on to the primed stone of the ceiling. The *walls* are covered with carved gilded limestone, and the unique *pavement* contains about 400 sepulchral memorials to the Order's aristocracy. Mazzuoli's great marble sculpture of the *Baptism of Christ* dominates the presbytery. The *altar* is made of lapis lazuli and other rare marbles. The side chapels were allotted to each of the "Langues" of the Order.

Zondadari's mausoleum to the left of the main entrance is worth noting as are those of the Cottoner brothers and Perellos in the Chapel of Aragon. There is also a beautiful *monument* by Pradier to the *Count of Beaujolais*, brother of Louis Philippe of France. The Grand Masters who died at Malta before the church was completed are buried in the **Crypt**.

During the month of June a superb set of *14 Flemish tapestries* are hung in the Church. During the year these are exhibited in the adjoining **Cathedral Museum** which also contains relics, religious vestments and the treasure of St John's. In the ornate *Oratory* is a painting by Caravaggio depicting the **Beheading of St John the Baptist**. This painting is regarded as Caravaggio's greatest masterpiece.

THE CHURCHES OF VALLETTA

The Knights of Malta were, and still are, a religious Order so it should be no surprise that Valletta has a considerable number of churches. **Our Lady of Mount Carmel**, for example, was built in 1570 by Gerolamo Cassar but was rebuilt after devastating bombing in 1942. Just as important is **St Paul's Anglican Cathedral** where the Gothic and neo-classical styles blend harmoniously. Standing opposite the 16th-century **church of St Catherine** is the **Church of Our Lady of Victory**, the first church to be built by the Knights in Valletta in 1566 to celebrate victory over the Turks. The **Church of St Paul's Shipwreck** houses sacred relics of the saint who was shipwrecked on the island in 60 AD. Lastly, in the suburb of **Floriana** just outside Valletta to the south-west forming a sort of natural extension of the city towards the interior of the island, is the majestic **Church of St Publius** with two towers and an elaborately decorated interior.

The impressive Church of Our Lady of Mount Carmel with its unmistakable lofty dome and, below, St Publius in Floriana.

REPUBLIC SQUARE, NATIONAL LIBRARY, ST JOHN'S SQUARE

Republic Square is also known by the older name of *Queen's Square* as it was originally named after Queen Victoria in 1897. An elegant *statue* of the queen dominates the centre of the square.

Overlooking it, with a façade of elegant arches, is the **National Library of Malta**, designed by Stefano Ittar, an architect from Calabria, and built between 1786 and 1796. Delayed by the French invasion, however, it was not opened until 1812. Today the library has some 61,000 volumes, 50 incunabula, 1250 illuminated manuscripts, the registers of the university from 1350 to 1818 and the precious archives of the Order (6,524 volumes dating from the 11th century on). **St John's Square** is also situated close to Republic Street. With its elegant porticos the square is also a delightful area of pleasant cafés and open-air bars.

Above, Republic Square, with its typical cafés and tables outside and, right, St John's Square.

THE GRAND MASTER'S PALACE

Valletta is a city of palaces but for the Maltese, the Grand Master's Palace is known simply as *il Palazz*, the Palace. The two main portals, baroque and imposing, stand in direct contrast to the unadorned treatment of the rest of the façade; three other side entrances lead to as many streets.

Three of the doorways open onto a spacious courtyard while another portal and a gate lead to a smaller courtyard on a slightly higher level. The larger of the two courtyards is known as the **Neptune Courtyard** after the bronze statue of the god there. The smaller courtyard - the **Prince Alfred Courtyard** - is named after one of Queen Victoria's sons to commemorate his visit to Malta in 1858, but it is better known as that of **Pinto's Clock**. This clock has four dials showing - besides the time - the day, the month and the phases of the moon. As in Renaissance palaces in Italy, the most important floor was the first, the **Piano Nobile**, the ground floor being used as stables, service quarters and stores. The **Main Staircase** leading up to the Piano Nobile was built by Grand Master Hughes de Loubenx Verdala, identified by the wolf in the coat of arms. The top of the

Above, the Grand Master's Palace and, on the left, the statue of Neptune. Facing page, a portrait of Grand Master Martin de Redin and a fresco in the Armoury Corridor.

staircase gives on to a lobby formed by the point where two of the palace corridors meet. The right-hand passage leads to what used to be the Palace **Armoury** but that part of the building is now the seat of the House of Representatives. The **Council**, or **Tapestry**, **Chamber** in the Armoury Corridor is an impressive hall where the members of the Order sat in Council. On being elected to office, a Grand Master was expected to make a gift to the Order - the Gioja. Part of the Gioja of Grand Master Ramon Perellos y Rocaful was the priceless set of **Gobelins Tapestries** that give the name to this chamber.

The first door to the right of the lobby leads into the **State Dining Room**. Here the British connection is well represented by several royal portraits.

The next door along the Entrance Corridor leads to the **Hall of the Supreme Council**, also known as

*In the corridor
leading to
what was
formerly the
Armoury is a
well-preserved
collection
of arms.*

the **Throne Room**. Like all the other ceilings of the Piano Nobile, the wooden ceiling of this hall is elaborately coffered and painted. Against the far end of the wall is the **throne**, occupied first by the Grand Masters and then by the British Governors. Above the throne now are the arms of the Republic of Malta. Across the hall and opposite the throne a carved **Minstrels' Gallery** is set into the wall; this carved and painted gallery is said to have been part of the Order's flagship, the Great Carrack of Rhodes, one of the vessels that carried the Knights to Malta. A door from the Throne Room leads to the **Ambassadors' Room**, also known as the **Red Room** from the colour of its damask hangings. A door from the Ambassadors' Room leads to the **Paggeria**, the Pages' Waiting Room, also known as the **Yellow Room** after the gold damask covering its walls. A door from the Pages' Waiting Room leads into a corridor which is at a right angle to the Entrance Corridor. This is known as the **Prince of Wales Corridor** in commemoration of a visit by King Edward VII, then Prince of Wales, in 1862. The rooms along this passage were formerly the **private apartment of the Grand Master**; later they were used as the offices of the British Governors. These rooms are now the offices of the President of the Republic.

The ground floor of the palace is now occupied by various government offices, including a number of Ministries, and what were previously the palace stables now house the Palace **Armoury**. The armoury was transferred to this part of the palace when the original Armoury was transformed to house the House of Representatives. As presently displayed, the collection of the **Armoury Museum** is small but interesting; in the old Armoury, and even more so in engravings of the Armoury as it once was, one is impressed by the

Paintings in the extensive picture gallery, pride of the Grand Master's Palace.

great number of exhibits, however, many of the specimens were repetitious and to the serious student a specimen collection is more interesting. At the time of the arrival of the Order in Malta, in 1530, the use of firearms was rapidly revolutionizing warfare - the Great Siege was fought largely with artillery and arquebuses but armour still had its uses. A century later breastplates and shields were still being tested against firearms, and in the Armoury there are several examples with dents in them to prove that they were "bulletproof". Another exhibit that combines the old and the new is a *sword* incorporating a wheel-lock pistol.

FORT ST ELMO

Where in the 15th century a watchtower stood, in 1551 the first fortress was built, and fifteen years later it managed to resist relentless bombardment by the Turks for an entire month. When it was finally taken all the occupants were massacred but by then it had become legendary. As a result Francesco Laparelli, an architect, was immediately commissioned to improve the defensive structures and the fort took on its present appearance, despite mainly superficial alterations and extensions carried out between the 17th and 18th centuries.

Currently, the Fort houses the island's **Police Academy** and the **National War Museum** where items relating to the Second World War are displayed including the only biplane to have survived the war.

Images that emphasise the solidity of the massive structure of Fort St Elmo showing also the original star-shaped plan; the National War Museum is now housed here.

NATIONAL WAR MUSEUM

The National War Museum was opened in part of Fort St Elmo in 1975. Thus, displayed in the old munitions deposit are some interesting exhibits from the time of the Second World War such as weapons and planes, and the jeep nicknamed "Husky" that escorted General Eisenhower and President Roosevelt around the island of Malta. Here too is the famous St George's Cross

presented by the king of England to the people of Malta for the courage they had shown. The gallery of photographs illustrating the sacrifices that the local population suffered is also extremely interesting.

Above, the Gloucester Gladiator, one of the airplanes exhibited in the Museum. Left, a room in the National War Museum in Fort St Elmo.

One of the most important events in the Maltese year, the **Carnival** was already recorded in 1535, but has been celebrated with particular enthusiasm since 1565 when, in song and dance, children represented the victory over the Turks.

On the Saturday before Lent there is a parade of grotesque figures through the streets of the city, followed by musicians in historic costume and, to permit the carnival floats to pass through, the main city gate has even been altered. A real treat and festival for tourists as well.

Malta is an island, the realm of fishermen, with a history of seafaring. It is no surprise therefore that one of the best known images of the island are the highly coloured **boats** which are derived from ancient Phoenician vessels. The **Luzzu** is the traditional fishing boat while the **Dghajsa** is not unlike the Venetian gondola, but more colourful, and was used for transporting people and goods. The **Dghajsa** is now only seen in the Grand Harbour. On the prow of these boats is the unmistakable *Eye of Osiris*, Phoenician in origin and a symbol of protection for seafarers.

St. Julian's

North of Sliema, this old fishing village developed around the Chapel of St Julian in an area where many of the Knights' hunting lodges were situated. Today this is a busy tourist area and seaside resort. St Julian's overlooks a delightful narrow bay and the coast road along this beautiful part of the shore is quite lovely.

The typical little narrow streets of the town wind up along the rise of the coast to reach the impressive **Spinola Palace** dominating the bay from on high and surrounded by magnificent gardens. The original building dated from 1688 and was the pleasant summer residence of Paolo Raffaello Spinola from Genoa, the bailiff (or administrator) of the Order. Its present appearance dates from the 18th century renovation carried out by Spinola's grandson and designed by the architect Carapecchia. St Julian's has many attractions including the *Casino* and the rough and **rocky coast** where, despite everything, unusual structures that are quite comfortable have been created, intended to make bathing easier and to enable visitors to sunbathe and relax. And here too, at the far end of the bay, is a genuine rarity for Malta – a tiny *beach* of fine golden and compact sand, a little corner of paradise resting in the sun and representing a spot much frequented by tourists, although its tiny size means that access has to be restricted.

A spectacular group of attractive modern and even futuristic constructions can be seen in the area of St Julian's, **Portomaso**. While its function is primarily touristic and residential, it also comprises offices and various services. Thus, facing right onto the sea, there is the *Portomaso Tower* which has become the highly visible symbol of this resort. One hundred metres high, with 22 floors, the Tower houses numerous offices and there is also a conference centre.

Paceville

Entirely devoted to entertainment, Paceville is quite a compact area not far from St Julian's and extremely well-known. It is no exaggeration to say that the most interesting night life of Malta takes place here in an amazing concentration of restaurants, pubs, discos and fashionable bars that are crowded all night long with bright multi-coloured lights illuminating the dark, while music of all kinds fills the air.

Paceville really comes to life after dusk sets in and most of the clubs do not close until after 4am and some even remain open until dawn.

The true centre of **Malta's nightlife**, Paceville's *discotheques* can boast a clientele that is both numerous and international. Many young people come to frequent the bars and clubs which are capable of satisfying all kinds of musical preferences and interests. Maltese nights echo with the beat and rhythms of the most diverse types of music, from hip hop to reggae and soul. But live music is not neglected and there are frequent performances of both rock and blues bands. Memorable nights of entertainment under the starry sky of the island of Malta.

*Generally called the "Three Cities", the towns extending towards Valletta, dividing the Grand Harbour into deep inlets, are known historically with different names but those most commonly used today are **Vittoriosa, Senglea** and **Cospicua**. Originally, Birgu (now Vittoriosa) developed. Shortly afterwards the neighbouring peninsula was also fortified with ramparts and began to thrive, eventually becoming known as Senglea City. The agglomeration that subsequently developed between Senglea and Birgu became known as Bormla and it became known as the "Cospicua" (the Notable City).*

VITTORIOSA

Of the Three Cities, Vittoriosa is not only the oldest and most easterly, but historically is also the most important. It was the first port of the island in chronological terms. When, shortly after arriving on the island, the Knights of Malta chose Birgu as their first capital, the town flourished rapidly. Even when, after the great Siege, the Knights transferred the centre of their operations to the new town of Valletta, Vittoriosa continued to remain for many years a bishopric and headquarters of the Inquisitor. Today, however, a detailed and thorough programme of restoration has returned the town to its original, historic splendour.

FORT ST ANGELO AND FORT RICASOLI

Two old and mighty fortresses still survive as evidence of Vittoriosa's strategic position; as well as Fort St Angelo, already described, nearby on the parallel peninsula further west, extending across Grand Harbour, is the 17th-century Fort Ricasoli, almost a twin structure that still retains its original impressive appearance.

FORT RINELLA

Fort Rinella is interesting from many points of view, but especially historically as this is one of the few Maltese forts not to have been built by the Knights of St John. It is in fact a Victorian fortress now famous for the gigantic cannon, known as the **Armstrong Cannon** that is lo-cated here. The British Royal Navy commissioned the cannon; it has a 450 mm calibre, is more than 9 metres long, and weighs 103.64 tonnes. The enormous mouth is capable of firing shells weighing a tonne at a distance of eight miles. A pair of these incredibly powerful cannons were located on Malta in fact, but proved also to be incredibly expensive as far as maintenance and effectiveness were concerned; one was situated to the east of Grand Harbour, and the other to the west of the Marsamxett port. It took three months of hard work in the autumn of 1882 to position the cannon at Fort Rinella.

Opposite page, Fort St Angelo (above) and Fort Ricasoli.
Below, the Armstrong Cannon.

One of the Knights' greatest and most constant worries was how to defend of the strategic position of the Three Cities and render them impregnable. It is no surprise therefore that in the 17th century it was decided to protect them by building a double stone wall, one external (the **Cottonera Lines**) and the other internal (the **Margarita Lines**). The aim of the project was to enclose within these walls a large area of protected land, capable of supporting some 40,000 people with livestock and food supplies in the case of siege.

SENGLEA

This is the most western of the three peninsulas forming the south eastern section of Grand Harbour which for a long time remained uninhabited. Between 1553 and 1557 a small village developed here, surrounded by parks and gardens and soon fortified by Grand Master Claude de la Sengle, for whom the town was then named. Having gloriously survived the Great Siege, Senglea continued to grow and prosper, developing into an attractive town. Centuries later, terrible bombing during air raids by the forces of the Axis destroyed Senglea. Reconstruction was carried out around the few monuments that had survived. The most outstanding of these, on *Triq il-Vitorja*, the main street of Senglea, is the **Church of St Filippo Neri**, a 16th-century structure refurbished several times in the course of the 17th century. The church of **Our Lady of Victories** was designed and built in the 17th century by Cassar. The church houses many works of art, including the much venerated statue of the Redeemer (*Ir-Redentur*) and the statue of Our Lady, also known as the "La

bambina", traditionally lead in procession on 8 September every year to solemnly commemorate the end of the Great Siege. Without any doubt one particularly pleasant feature of Senglea is the small but delightful **public garden** (*Safe Haven Gardens*), located on the ramparts from where there is a stupendous panorama of Valletta and the port.

One of the most famous attractions of Senglea is the hexagonal watchtower which dominates the Safe Haven Gardens with its original sculpted decoration.

Typical views of Cospicua: above, the entrance on the south, Port St Elena;
left, a shining statue of the Virgin, much venerated in Cospicua
and in the Three Cities in general.

COSPICUA

Protected by a massive stone wall and by the two peninsulas of Senglea and Vittoriosa that encircle its bay, the town first came into being as a small fishing village, for long known as *Bormla* until it was given its current impressive name by Grand Master Marcantonio Zondadari who, during the first half of the 18th century, decided to commemorate the courage shown by the inhabitants during the Great Siege of 1565 with this title.

For a long period the town's fortunes depended on the busy naval dockyards at the end of *Dockyard Creek* where originally galley boats were produced and later modern ships of heavy tonnage. It was precisely because of these shipyards that Cospicua became the target of heavy bombing during the Second World War.

Today, with 10,000 inhabitants, Cospicua is a densely populated and flourishing town, one of the most important industrial centres on Malta, although the narrow medieval streets and the mighty defensive walls enclosing it might seem little suited to accommodate modern industrial development. Among its most important monuments are the baroque **Church of the Immaculate Conception** (16th-century but refurbished on several occasions) and the 17th-century **Church of St Teresa of Avila**.

The Megalithic Temples of Malta and Gozo

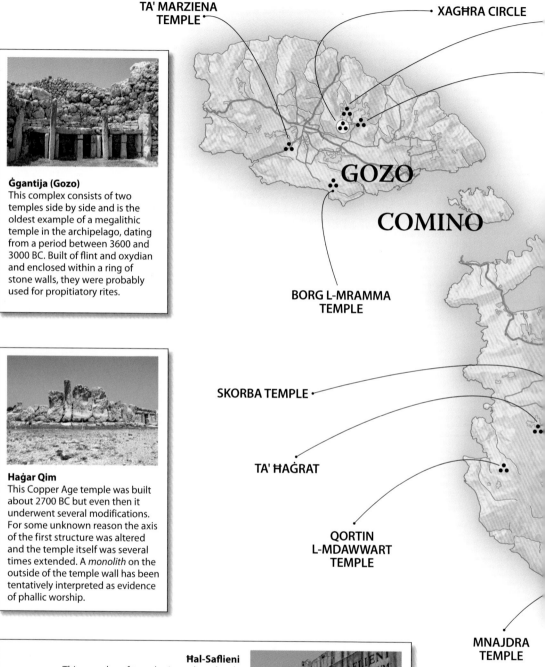

TA' MARZIENA TEMPLE

XAGĦRA CIRCLE

GOZO

COMINO

BORG L-MRAMMA TEMPLE

SKORBA TEMPLE

TA' ĦAĠRAT

QORTIN L-MDAWWART TEMPLE

MNAJDRA TEMPLE

Ġgantija (Gozo)
This complex consists of two temples side by side and is the oldest example of a megalithic temple in the archipelago, dating from a period between 3600 and 3000 BC. Built of flint and oxydian and enclosed within a ring of stone walls, they were probably used for propitiatory rites.

Ħaġar Qim
This Copper Age temple was built about 2700 BC but even then it underwent several modifications. For some unknown reason the axis of the first structure was altered and the temple itself was several times extended. A *monolith* on the outside of the temple wall has been tentatively interpreted as evidence of phallic worship.

Ħal-Saflieni
This complex of temples is on three levels underground reaching a depth of 12 metres. Built in different stages from 3000 to 2000 BC, Ħal-Saflieni is noted for a spiral staircase that is surprizingly modern both in form and concept. The most interesting rooms are on the second level, such as the *Oracle Room* and the *Holy of Holies*.

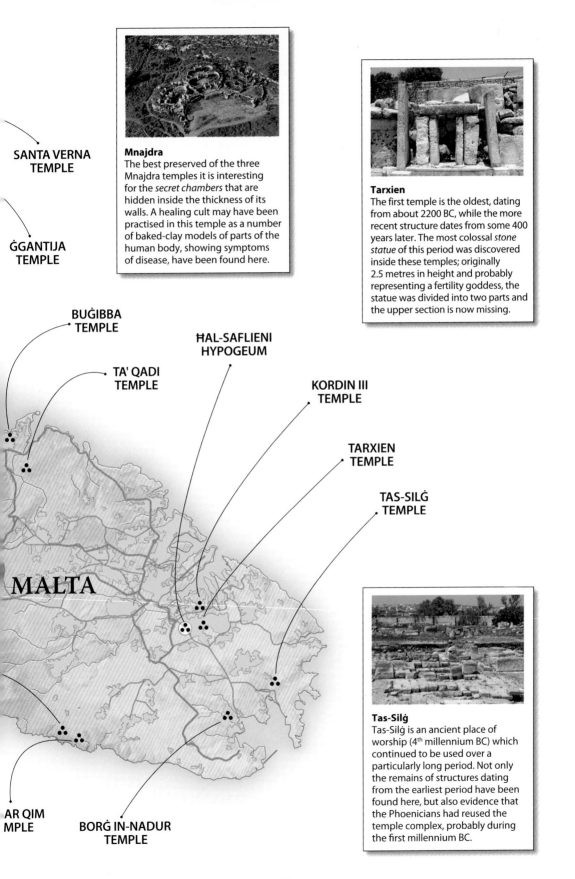

SANTA VERNA TEMPLE

ĠGANTIJA TEMPLE

Mnajdra
The best preserved of the three Mnajdra temples it is interesting for the *secret chambers* that are hidden inside the thickness of its walls. A healing cult may have been practised in this temple as a number of baked-clay models of parts of the human body, showing symptoms of disease, have been found here.

Tarxien
The first temple is the oldest, dating from about 2200 BC, while the more recent structure dates from some 400 years later. The most colossal *stone statue* of this period was discovered inside these temples; originally 2.5 metres in height and probably representing a fertility goddess, the statue was divided into two parts and the upper section is now missing.

BUĠIBBA TEMPLE

ĦAL-SAFLIENI HYPOGEUM

TA' QADI TEMPLE

KORDIN III TEMPLE

TARXIEN TEMPLE

TAS-SILĠ TEMPLE

MALTA

AR QIM MPLE

BORĠ IN-NADUR TEMPLE

Tas-Silġ
Tas-Silġ is an ancient place of worship (4th millennium BC) which continued to be used over a particularly long period. Not only the remains of structures dating from the earliest period have been found here, but also evidence that the Phoenicians had reused the temple complex, probably during the first millennium BC.

Għar Dalam

A real natural gem, the cave of Għar Dalam is on the coast not far from Birżebbugia. *Fossilized bones of animals* have been discovered in caves and fissures in various parts of the island, but the largest concentration to be discovered so far is that at Għar Dalam.

In 1917 two human molars were found in this cave and, at the time of their discovery were believed to be those of Neanderthal Man.

However, these molars have now been assigned to a much later period.

Illustrated here are the grotto and museum of Għar Dalam and views of Marsaxlokk: Fort St Lucian, the Sunday market, the Church of Our Lady of Pompei and some luzzus.

Marsaxlokk

Marsaxlokk, the harbour to the south-east, is now a small but picturesque harbour where the brightly coloured fishing boats ride at anchor and where the wives of the fishermen knot nylon string bags for the tourists. But Marsaxlokk is also a microcosm of the historical past of the island. A short distance from this village is the archaeological site of *Tas-Silġ* still in the process of being excavated; the remains of Late Neolithic megalithic buildings have been found here, greatly modified by superimposed Punic and Byzantine structures; here too are the

The Sunday market

The port of Marsaxlokk is strongly identified with its traditional activities and is also famous for the crowded market which takes place here every Sunday.

As might be expected, this is principally a fish market, held right on the seafront but close also to a general market where there are many stalls displaying numerous varieties and types of lace.

only remains of a mosque to be found on the island. Norman coins have also been found at Tas-Silġ. To prevent the landing of corsairs in the harbour, *Fort St Lucian* was erected at its entrance by the Order. Marsaxlokk Bay, of which the fishing harbour of Marsaxlokk forms part, is now being converted into a port for container ships.

Marsaxlokk is widely known for its traditional boats "with eyes", the **luzzu**; it is traditionally believed that these eyes (of ancient Phoenician origin) protect the boats from danger.

*Attractive views of the Blue Grotto
and the rocky coast
around Wied iż-Żurrieq.*

Wied iż-Żurrieq and the Blue Grotto

The western coast of Malta is steep and precipitous but in places clefts in the cliffs slope down to sea-level. One such cleft is Wied iż-Żurrieq. Another attraction of this area is the **Blue Grotto**.

The presence of this deep sea-cave, in which the sea depths are of an unbelievably intense blue, has long been known to the fisher folk. During World War II, when an air-raid alarm was sounded the inhabitants took to their boats and rowed into the cave for safety.

Dingli

Standing at a height of 250 metres, this village offers a magnificent panorama: the sea, the small island of Filfla and the Buskett Gardens are all visible from here. Not far from this little village are the **Dingli Cliffs**, which look truly impressive especially when seen from the sea. A small *chapel*, built in honour of Mary Magdalene stands here and also indicates the highest point of the island. The slopes of the hillsides are terraced for agricultural production.

Verdala Palace and Buskett Gardens

The Verdala Palace in Buskett is now used by the president of the Republic for representation purposes and heads of state on official visit are housed here. Designed in 1586 by Gerolamo Cassar (who also designed St John's Co-Cathedral), it was built for the Grand Master and cardinal Hughes de Loubenx Verdala as a country villa surrounded by beautiful gardens. The countryside all around was called *Buskett*, from the Italian word "boschetto" meaning woods. The villa is constructed on a base surrounded by a moat which is crossed by a flight of stairs. These lead to the ground floor where there is a spacious stairway, famous for its vault decorated with frescoes portraying the achievements of the

Grand Master. A lovely elliptical stair leads to the first floor. A *chapel*, dedicated to St Anthony Abbot, where a painting by Preti is housed, is located in the Buskett Gardens where cypresses, oaks, pines and ashes thrive as well as orange and lemon trees, the fruits of which are gathered and sold during the Christmas period. A competition of ballad-singers, known as the *ghanja*, is held in the garden every year.

Rabat incorporates much of the old Roman city which was reduced to its present dimensions by the Arabs. The Rabat area is closely connected with the introduction of Christianity to the islands: in 60 AD St Paul the Apostle, under arrest on his way to Rome, was shipwrecked on the island. Today, besides schools and colleges, Rabat has various social clubs and musical bands, a market which is very popular on Sunday mornings, and sports fields. The area around Rabat is ideal for walks in the countryside.

RABAT

St Paul's Collegiate Church is constructed upon, but to the left of **St Paul's Grotto**, just outside the walls and in the ditch of the old city, hence reference to it as St Paul Outside The Walls in old documents. The dedication to St Paul is due to the traditional belief that St Paul used the cave as a base for his preaching and to create a Christian community during his three months' stay in Malta in 60 AD. For this reason St Paul's Grotto was described by the Cathedral Chapter as "the foundation stone of the Church in Malta". Grand Master Alof de Wignacourt transformed the church into a Collegiate of the Order, constructed a col-

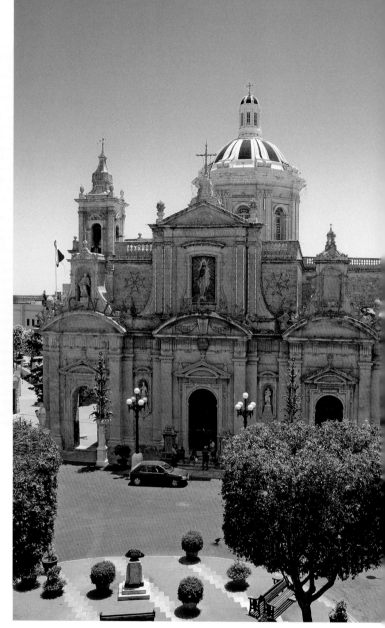

St Paul's Collegiate Church and, opposite, two views of St Paul's Grotto, a catacombe housing a touching statue of the saint.

lege for chaplains officiating the new institution and erected a College as well as a new *church of St Publius*, adjacent to St Paul's Parish Church. The Order of St. John enriched the building with various works of art, including a fine altarpiece with St Publius by Mattia Preti, an altarpiece of the *Eucharist* by Francesco Zahra (1710-1773), a *statue of St Paul* over the altar in the Grotto by the Maltese sculptor Melchiorre Gafà

and a fine 18th-century Neapolitan organ by Giuseppe del Piano. Among its works of art are three paintings by Stefano Erardi (1630-1716) and the huge altarpiece by Francesco Zahra of the *Holy Family* for a side altar. From Preti's workshop are *The Stoning of St Stephen* in the transept, *St Michael* and the oval depicting *God the Father* in the chapel on the right of the entrance.

MUSEUM OF ROMAN ANTIQUITIES

The misnamed "Roman Villa" Museum covers the site of a rich and sumptuously decorated town house that once belonged to a wealthy person in Roman Malta. The site, discovered in 1881 and further excavated in 1920-24, contains a number of remarkably fine **mosaic polychrome pavements** and some original architectural elements. A number of rooms were constructed

The Museum of Roman Antiquities and one of the mosaics housed there. Below, a view of St Agatha Catacombs.

to protect the mosaics and an upper hall was added to provide exhibition space and a suitable entrance.

The porticoed neo-classical façade was completed in 1925. The *mosaics* offer the main attraction, rated among the finest and oldest in the western Mediterranean.

ST AGATHA CATACOMBS

Not far from St Paul's Grotto, below the church of St Agatha, are spectacular catacombs dedicated to the saint and covering some 4,000 square metres, though only a very small area can be visited.

The walls are decorated with numerous frescoes dating from the 12th to the 15th centuries, Byzantine in style and portraying scenes from the life of the Saint who is traditionally believed to have passed part of her exile on Malta.

A small *museum* is situated beside the catacombs, displaying a wide range of antique objects including ceramics, clothing and coins.

MDINA

The Arabs divided the old Roman city of Melita into two: the citadel became known as Mdina *(the city)* and the rest of the area as Rabat *(the suburb)*, names which are still used today. In medieval times Mdina was the seat of municipal government and an important administrative centre. There are many beautiful buildings and monuments in this small city, including in particular the 18*th* century **Vilhena Palace** (or the **Grand Masters' Palace**) now housing the Museum of Natural History and the elegant palaces of **Villegaignon Street**, as well as of course, the impressive and austere **Cathedral**.

THE CATHEDRAL

Above, the Expulsion from Eden *by Bernardo Strozzi exhibited in the Cathedral Museum in Mdina; below, the interior of the dome of St. Mary's church in Mosta (right, the exterior).*

According to tradition, the first Cathedral of Malta was dedicated to the Blessed Virgin, but, having fallen into ruin during the Muslim period, it was rebuilt following the Norman conquest and re-dedicated to St Paul. The dreadful earthquake of 11 January 1693 almost entirely destroyed the cathedral and only the sacristy and choir, which had both been recently built, were left standing. Construction of a larger building in baroque style began immediately and the Maltese architect Lorenzo Gafà was commissioned for the task. The new cathedral was completed and consecrated in 1702.

CATHEDRAL MUSEUM

On Archbishop's Square, the Cathedral Museum has been located in a baroque palace since 1969 and contains extensive artistic and archaeological collections as well as important archives. The most substantial part of the *artistic collections* comes from the legacy of Count Saverio Marchese (1757-1833). A large room is used for the temporary exhibition of new acquisitions.

Mosta

Mosta is roughly in the geographical centre of the island of Malta. Given its position, Mosta is an important crossroads lying on the route for those travelling from the south and the east towards the north of the island.

The chief attraction is now the monumental church, dedicated to the Assumption and called **St Mary's**, with its circular design which was inspired by the Pantheon in Rome. Its *dome* is the third largest in Europe, the two other domes being in Rome and in London. The building was started in 1833 and the church was consecrated in 1871; it was built around and over an earlier church which continued to be used during the period when work was in progress. Like many other of the old churches in Malta therefore, this is a true monument of faith.

Today one of the main items of interest in the Church of St Mary is attributed to a great miracle worked through the divine intercession of the Virgin. Exhibited in the sacristy is the fearful bomb that, at 16.40 on 9 April 1942, crashed through the dome, bounced off the walls twice inside before coming to rest on the floor without exploding. Two others simply grazed the church and rolled into the square in front also without exploding. Hundreds of worshippers were attending Mass at the time, yet no one was injured.

St. Paul's Bay

The town which was once a small fishing port is now a well-known tourist and seaside resort. Its history is linked to the life of St Paul who landed here in 60 AD following a shipwreck. It was here that he quenched his thirst (and it is still possible to visit *Għajn Rażul*, the *Apostle's Fountain*); here it is believed the saint threw the snake into the fire (where today the *Church of tal-Ħuġġieġa* or church of the bonfire now stands); and here the Roman governor Publius welcomed him (the *Church of San Pawl Milqghi* records this event). Yet the present and the future of this area are determined by an ever-increasing and constant tourism. Thus the large bay in the area to the south west (known as **Xemxija**) is a continuous series of residential zones linking St Paul's Bay to lively **Buġibba** and elegant **Qawra**.

Two views of splendid Buġibba.

Mellieħa

On old maps, two landmarks are indicated to the north of Malta: the salt marshes, and the old church of Mellieħa. The production of salt has been moved elsewhere (the old salt works were once sited where the *Għadira Bird Sanctuary* now stands), but the old partially **underground church dedicated to Our Lady** still stands here. According to tradition, a *fresco of the Virgin Mary* was painted by the apostle St. Luke who, with St. Paul, was shipwrecked near here in the year 60 AD. Scientific study of the icon has assigned it to a more recent, but still quite ancient, period.

Għadira Nature Reserve

In the north west of Malta, at the end of Mellieħa Bay, lies a marshy area of ponds where all the rain water that falls locally collects due to the morphological structure of the area. They form a fantastic natural landscape where a nature reserve, called Għadira ("salt marshes"), has been located since the 1960s. This entire area rapidly developed into a safe and comfortable refuge for many endemic reptiles, insects and small mammals. Of the many creatures that inhabit the pools some of the most fascinating are the gecko, the Mediterranean chameleon, the weasel, wild rabbits and bats. With the passing of time, however, and as a result of its particular environmental features, Għadira has increasingly become mainly a true sanctuary for wild birds.

The entire north and south-west coast of the island of Malta is formed by an uninterrupted series of bays, some deep, some broad and peaceful, creating a magnificent and fascinating landscape. Swept by the waves of a crystal sea, looking even more impressive with the wild rocky slopes that rise just behind the coastline, bear and rugged in appearance, these inlets are isolated and beautiful with an air of natural severity that makes them seem almost timeless. Yet it is not difficult to reach them as they are served by convenient roads and efficient bus routes and nearby several large tourist structures have developed. To the north west, for example, just in front of the island of Gozo is the peaceful little **Paradise Bay**.

Nearby **Anchor Bay** is pretty and unspoiled and its clear waters with an abundance of fish have made it particularly popular with skin divers, though it also was made famous by the film director, Robert Altman who had an unusual village built here for the set of his film, "Popeye".

Continuing south along the coast is **Golden Bay** with its blue green sea and fine, firm and golden sand, as well as **Għajn Tuffieħa Bay**; both can be reached on foot by long flights of steps and are well connected to Valletta by bus and to St Paul's Bay by a convenient road that crosses one of the most fertile and luxuriant parts of the island.

Yet further south is **Ġnejna Bay**, surrounded by imposing rock faces but with a splendid beach almost 300 metres long, and providing a peaceful refuge for those who wish to enjoy the sea and sun surrounded by the silence of nature. High above the *Lippia Tower*, an 17th-century watch tower built by Grand Master Lascaris, seems to be watching over the safety of the bathers.

One of the most intriguing amusement parks on the island of Malta is **Sweethaven**, the almost fairytale village of Popeye, created in Anchor Bay in 1979 as the set of the film made by Robert Altman recounting the adventures of the brawny sailor and his inseparable Olive Oil. Altogether 17 highly original little houses were made by teams of labourers with wood brought from Canada and the Netherlands for the purpose. When shooting of the film came to an end they were converted into an amusement park that is truly unique. Here children enter the magical world of Popeye where they can participate in shows and games, travel on a miniature train, experience the thrill of a mini-rollercoaster – and be photographed with the characters of this most famous cartoon strip.

GOZO

Malta's smaller sister island is different in that it is more fertile and more picturesque, but what makes Gozo so markedly different from Malta are the Gozitans. These frugal and tough people seem resistant to any adversity; their character is steel-like, tempered by privations and constant danger and, as a result of their frequent ordeals, they and their descendants have emerged strong and resilient. Malta and Gozo share the same history and similar historical remains are found on both islands, but Gozo has had more than its share of misfortunes. Largely undefended, the island has many times been devastated by pirate attacks. When Gozitans had advance warning of an impending invasion, such as the Great Siege, some of them sought refuge in the better fortified towns of Malta while the elderly were evacuated to Sicily, but they always returned home as soon as it was safe for them to do so. Gozitans ransomed from slavery also returned home, never thinking of nor wishing to settle in a safer place. Perhaps what makes Gozo special is the love and quiet pride of its inhabitants for their homeland and this pride is reflected, among other things, in the size and beauty of their churches.

The love that Gozitans have for their homeland is contagious too. Many visitors have been fascinated by the island and have decided to remain, becoming Gozitans themselves (except for Ulysses who, after staying for seven years, renounced the charms of the nymph Calypso, who, it is said, lived on Gozo). Rural and romantic, perhaps – but not uncultured: opera singers of international fame are often invited to perform in the capital of Gozo, Victoria. Younger generations enjoy concerts by pop singers and the music festivals. Moreover, some of Malta's best brains come from Gozo.

Mġarr

The port of Mġarr is the foremost point of access to Gozo, where the ferries from Malta dock. And indeed the word *mgarr* can mean equally "market place" or "departure point". The neo-gothic **Church of Our Lady of Lourdes** was built in 1888 high on the hill that overlooks the main port and the more recent tourist marina and appears to welcome the boats as they arrive. On the left, at the top of the unmistakable blue-grey cliffs and also seeming to protect the quays and wharfs below, is the impressive *Fort Chambray* which was planned during the 1600s but only built in 1749 by the governor of Gozo, Jacques de Chambray. It was therefore the last fortification made by the Knights and valiantly succeeded in blocking invasion by the French after strong resistance to their advance in 1798.

Discovering the bays and beaches of Calypso's island

The small but delightful island of Gozo is noted for the beauty of its many little known and generally unspoilt corners as well as for its singular geological features.

Amidst the impressive cliffs and natural pools of salt water there are magnificent inlets such as the splendid **Dwejra Bay** to the west with its amazing crystal clear water (pages 60-61 showing, below, the natural arch nearby known as the "Blue Window"), and **Xlendi Bay**, one of the few where the recent success of tourism can be seen (above left). But there are also genuine small fjords, often etched out over the centuries by the sea, or that have developed along the fault lines of Malta (called *wied*), such as the inviting **Mġarr ix-Xini** (left) and the **Ta' Ċenċ Cliffs** (right).

Fungus Rock

This cliff, over 50 metres high, is named *"Gebla tal-General"* (the General's Rock) by the locals as it is said that a Commander of the Order of St John discovered a *shrub* here which is known locally as *"Gherq Sinjur"* (*Cynomorium coccineum* Linn.). The plant was jealously protected by the Knights of St John as it was believed to possess great medicinal properties against certain ailments and illnesses. In 1744 Grand Master Pinto rendered the rock completely inaccessible. Until the middle of the last century the Government employed a guardian for Fungus Rock.

Ramla Bay. Opposite, the Qbajjar salt marshes,
a bay on Gozo and Calypso's Grotto.

One of Gozo's many attractions, in addition to the cliffs formed by the sea and the winds and the stupendous isolated beaches (the red beach of **Ramla Bay** is the most famous of the island), are the characteristic *salt marshes*, basins of salt water usually linked to the sea by long tunnels, and **Calypso's Grotto** of legendary fame. According to tradition, Gozo is identified as the island of Ogygia, where the nymph Calypso kept Ulysses for seven years, promising him immortality if he were to stay with her forever. Zeus intervened however, forbidding this destiny and Ulysses departed. Although it is difficult to compare the current state of the grotto and its surroundings with Homer's description of Calypso's residence in the *Odyssey*, prehistoric terracotta remains dating from the Ġgantija period (c. 3600 BC), have been found just a few metres from the cave entrance.

Victoria (Rabat)

The Gozitans always use the name of *Rabat*; it is the only town in Gozo and was named Victoria in 1897. It is in the centre of the island and has been the capital of Gozo probably since Roman times.

The Romans built defensive walls around the town which the Arabs continued to reinforce after conquering the island in 870 AD. Nothing structurally very old has survived but in the haphazard, twisting lanes and alley-ways of the town, splendid balconies and grand palaces revealing features of local architecture are still to be seen. Visitors will find a wide range of items in the many small shops and markets throughout Victoria.

THE CITADEL

The original nucleus of Victoria, the Citadel, is built on one of the many flat-topped hills in the centre of Gozo. Its origins can be traced to the late Middle Ages.

The *walls* themselves date from the 16th to the 18th centuries. Most of the buildings inside the Citadel are in ruins but the **Old Courts of Law** and the **Old Governor's Palace** are still being used as the Law Courts of Gozo. The **Old Prisons** and the **Armoury of the Knights**, the **Archaeological**, **Natural History** and **Folklore Museums** can all be visited.

The **Cathedral**, together with the **Bishop's Palace** and the **Cathedral Museum**, dominates the Citadel.

The ancient Citadel, with its imposing fortified enclosure, overlooks not only the city of Victoria. In the south east is the Cathedral dedicated to the Virgin Mary; below, its façade is particularly elegant in its tranquil simplicity.

Above, the cathedral interior, the entrance to the Folklore Museum and on the right, the Majmuna tombstone housed in the Archaeological Museum.

THE CATHEDRAL

The Cathedral designed by the Maltese architect Lorenzo Gafà in the form of a Latin cross was built between 1697 and 1711 on the site of an older church. Inside, one's attention is drawn instantly to the trompe l'oeil *ceiling* depicting the interior of a dome painted by Antonio Manuele of Messina in 1739. Paintings by the Maltese artists Giuseppe Hyzler, Michele Busuttil and Tommaso Madiona are also found here. Equally interesting are the *high altar* inlaid with precious malachite and, on either side of the main door, the pair of *baptismal fonts* sculpted from blocks of Gozo onyx.

The Ta' Pinu Sanctury and on the left, the Xewkija Rotonda. Opposite page, the church of St Lawrence and a view of Marsalforn.

Ta' Pinu Sanctuary

This is a national shrine and a centre of pilgrimage for both the Gozitans and the Maltese. The present **church** was begun in 1920 and was consecrated in 1931. It was raised to the status of basilica by Pope Pius XI a year later. The old *chapel* with the original painting can still be seen at the very end of the church where votive offerings are hung on either side of the shrine.

Xewkija

The **church** of Xewkija is dedicated to St John the Baptist and its **dome** is one of the largest in the world. Building was begun in 1952 and was completed in 1973. Besides an *altar panel* by Giacchino Loretta, a pupil of Mattia Preti, there are three excellent *works* by Francesco Zahra.

Sannat

Sannat is the most southerly village of the island. The **church**, dedicated to St Margaret, was built in 1718 to replace a smaller one after Sannat had become a parish in 1688. The main *altar panel* was made by Stefano Erardi. Another important work is the *St Francis altar panel* by Francesco Zahra. Going to the left of the church, at the top of the hill, **Ta' Ċenċ** is famous for its cliffs.

Marsalforn

This is the best known holiday resort on Gozo and the harbour is always busy, especially in summertime. Originally a fishing port, the colourful boats can still be seen in a sheltered corner of the bay. All kinds of marine sports can be enjoyed here and, in addition, Marsalforn has an attractive sandy beach with hotels, bed and breakfast, apartments and shops that are well stocked with souvenirs.

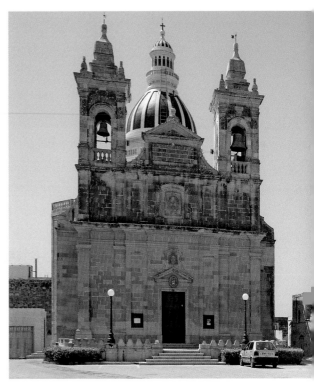

COMINO AND COMINOTTO

For long periods of its history **Comino** was an unsafe place in which to live. Nevertheless, people did inhabit this tiny island lying between Malta and Gozo at various times, and the population fluctuated from zero to just a few inhabitants.

In 1416 the Maltese petitioned the Aragonese king, Alphonse V, to build a tower on Comino as a deterrent to the corsairs who made it their base, but the people of the island had to wait two hundred years before work began and the Tower of Comino was only finally finished under Grand Master Alof de Wignacourt in 1618.

Despite the protection of the tower, people were wary of making Comino their home and the ancient church here was, in fact, deconsecrated in 1667 as it was derelict; in 1716 it was repaired and reconsecrated and by this time the island had been repopulated to some extent.

With its handful of resident families and a single hotel, even now the atmosphere and landscape on Comino is that of a deserted but very beautiful island.

Uninhabited and bare, the little island of **Cominotto** is immediately to the west of nearby Comino; the two islands are separated by a small channel, named the **Blue Lagoon** for its amazingly blue and crystalline waters.

In 1993 much of the channel was closed to shipping to make it a pleasant and relaxing spot for bathing.